MEDIEVAL WARFARE

Knights and Armor

By Deborah Murrell

WITHDRAWN

WORLD ALMANAC® LIBRARY

Please visit our web site at www.garethstevens.com
For a free color catalog describing Gareth Stevens Publishing's
list of high-quality books call 1-800-542-2595 (USA)
or 1-800-387-3178 (Canada).
Gareth Stevens Publishing's fax: 1-877-542-2596

Library of Congress Cataloging-in-Publication Data

Murrell, Deborah Jane, 1963–
        Knights and Armor / Deborah Murrell.
                    p. cm. — (Medieval Warfare)
            Includes bibliographical references and index.
        ISBN-13: 978-0-8368-9210-9 (lib. bdg.)
        ISBN-10: 0-8368-9210-0 (lib. bdg.)
        ISBN-13: 978-0-8368-9337-3 (softcover)
        ISBN-10: 0-8368-9337-9 (softcover)
        1. Knights and knighthood—Europe—juvenile literature.
2. Civilization, medieval—juvenile literature.   3. Armor—Europe—history—juvenile
literature.   I. title.
CR4513.M875 2008
940.1—DC22   2008016836

This North American edition first published in 2009 by

World Almanac® Library
An Imprint of Gareth Stevens Publishing
1 Reader's Digest Road
Pleasantville, NY 10570-7000 USA

Copyright © 2009 by Amber Books, Ltd.
Produced by Amber Books Ltd., Bradley's Close
74–77 White Lion Street
London N1 9PF, U.K.

All illustrations © Amber Books, Ltd. except:
AKG Images: 6, 12tl; Board of the Trustees of the Armouries: 7tl & br, 22; Bridgeman
Art Library: 15 (Bibliotheque de L'Arsenal/Archives Charmet), 29 (Bibliotheque
Nationale); Corbis: 8 (The Gallery Collection), 9 (Art Archive), 25 (Gianni Dagli Orti);
DK Images: 12–13; Getty Images: 16bl, 29; Heritage Image Partnership: 10, 11, 16tr,
and 28; Mars: 3; Topfoto: 4, 20, 23, 26

Amber Project Editor: James Bennett
Amber Designer: Joe Conneally

Gareth Stevens Senior Managing Editor: Lisa M. Herrington
Gareth Stevens Editor: Joann Jovinelly
Gareth Stevens Creative Director: Lisa Donovan
Gareth Stevens Designer: Paul Bodley

Printed in the United States of America

1 2 3 4 5 6 7 8 9 10 09 08

Contents

CHAPTER 1

Knights in the Middle Ages

The Middle Ages, also known as the Medieval period, was a time of constant fighting in Europe. Kingdom fought kingdom. Lord fought lord for land and power. The Normans, a people led by William the Conqueror, were the largest and most successful group. The Middle Ages began around A.D. 476 and lasted roughly 1,000 years. The era ended in 1453, when the Hundred Years' War between England and France was over. During this time, the countries of Europe began to form.

Types of Soldiers

Most of the soldiers in a medieval army were ordinary people. They fought on foot. Poor foot soldiers had only farm tools, such as axes, as weapons. They wore no

A single piece of armor protected the horse's face and eyes.

Armor plates were joined together loosely so the horse could move its neck.

◄ KNIGHT AND HORSE ARMOR
A knight whose horse was killed in battle would no longer be able to charge with the other knights. He would have to fight on foot. Not all knights had armor for their horses.

The horse's chest was protected by strong armor. A blow to its organs would be deadly.

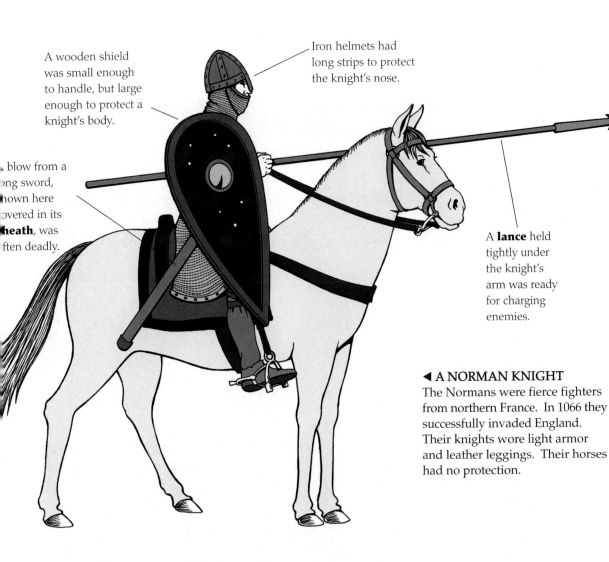

A wooden shield was small enough to handle, but large enough to protect a knight's body.

Iron helmets had long strips to protect the knight's nose.

blow from a ong sword, hown here overed in its **heath**, was ften deadly.

A **lance** held tightly under the knight's arm was ready for charging enemies.

◄ A NORMAN KNIGHT
The Normans were fierce fighters from northern France. In 1066 they successfully invaded England. Their knights wore light armor and leather leggings. Their horses had no protection.

armor or other protection. **Nobles**, or lords, were much richer. They owned land and could afford to fight on horseback. They wore armor to war and carried the best weapons. Nobles who fought on horseback were called **knights**.

Knights were the celebrities of the Middle Ages. Some became famous in songs and poems. It was the knights (and princes and kings) who people wrote about when they described great deeds on the battlefield. Sometimes, kings made a

soldier a knight after a brave fight. But usually knights came from the richest noble families. The knights had years of training. It took a lot of money to train a knight and buy a horse and armor.

Training to Be a Knight

Becoming a knight began early in life for boys from noble families. Young boys often lived in neighboring households during their training. These trainee knights, called **pages**, often began such training at age

▼ KNIGHTS AND SQUIRES

Squires cleaned and fixed a knight's weapons and helped them prepare for battle. Here, each squire attaches a sword onto his knight's belt. The knights hold their arms up out of the way.

seven. They served the lord and lady and were taught manners and basic fighting skills. Pages first practiced swordfighting using wooden swords. Early riding lessons often took place on a wooden horse, rather than a real one. Some pages also had to learn Latin taught by a **chaplain**, a priest who lived with the family.

By age 14, if a page had completed training, he was expected to become a **squire**. Squires practiced more advanced fighting skills, such as swinging a sword

◄ HELMET
This helmet completely covered the knight's head. The front **visor** could be lifted so the knight could see and speak clearly. Chain mail also protected the head.

▼ HAUBERK
Chain mail tunics (long shirts) were called **hauberks**. Knights had to be strong—a hauberk like this weighed more than 22 pounds (10 kilograms).

Sleeves were short so the heavy mail did not weigh down a knight's arms when he fought.

The metal rings were linked together, which allowed knights to fight and move normally.

while riding a galloping horse. Squires acted as assistants to knights and traveled with them. Squires took care of their knights' armor and weapons. **Chain mail** (armor consisting of hundreds of tiny metal rings) rusted easily. A knight's chain mail had to be regularly rolled in sand to remove the rust. Squires also helped knights look after their horses. They helped knights put on their armor.

The hauberk was designed to be worn on horseback, so its botttom edge was split.

A Knight's Horses

Knights had more than one horse. Sometimes they had different types of horses for different tasks. Lightweight horses, such as the palfrey (PALL-free), or trotting horse, might carry a knight to a battle. But for fighting, many knights changed to heavier, stronger horses that could carry them and their armor. These horses were called destriers (DES-tree-urs). Other knights used lighter horses called coursers in battle. These lighter horses were often less expensive than destriers.

▲ **KNIGHTS IN BATTLE**
Christian knights in this illustration are shown fighting Muslim horsemen. This battle took place during the **Crusades**—wars fought between Christians and Muslims during the Middle Ages.

DID YOU KNOW?

Medieval knights often had long hair. When they twisted it up underneath their helmet, it made useful padding. The hair softened the effect of a blow on the head, like a modern riding helmet does.

Becoming a Knight

Most squires served their masters for seven years, until age 21. Then they hoped to be made into knights. Only a king or prince, or another knight, could promote a squire to knight. In some kingdoms, squires had to go through **rituals** before they were knighted. One such ritual required squires to pray for an entire night. The basic ceremony consisted of the king or knight tapping the squire on his shoulders and head with an armored glove called a **gauntlet**. The king then **pronounced** the squire a knight. This was called "dubbing."

▼ DUBBING
In this medieval illustration the king is dubbing a knight with his gauntlet. The dubbing ceremony was followed by a grand celebration, often with games and mock duels.

The king made the squire a knight by touching him on the shoulder with his gauntlet.

Kneeling in front of the king, the squire promised to obey him.

The king's army watched the squire become a knight.

CHAPTER 2

The Feudal System

In the Middle Ages, people in Europe lived under the **feudal system**. Under this system, the king officially owned all the land in the kingdom. The king gave pieces of land, or estates, to his nobles to rule. An estate ruled by a noble was called a **fief**. The barons and knights who ruled the fiefs were known as **vassals** of the king. In order to become a vassal and be given a fief, the noble had to swear an oath to the king. He had to promise that he would be loyal to the king and fight for him.

Sworn Loyalty

Nobles often granted smaller fiefs to lesser nobles, who became their vassals. Again, lesser nobles had to promise their loyalty to the higher noble

and fight for him. When a vassal did not want to fight, he paid a fee instead. The king or noble might then use the money to hire a professional soldier called a **mercenary** to fight in his place.

▶ A KNIGHT AND A PEASANT
This painting shows a knight in full armor alongside a peasant who is sweeping the floor.

Nobles who were granted a fief lived on and farmed the land. Farming was done by peasants, or working people, called **serfs**. Serfs were allowed to farm part of the land for their own needs as payment for providing the lord with food and labor. If serfs were not given an area to farm for themselves, they were given a portion of the food they produced. Men, women, and children all tended the fields, especially at harvest time. An overseer, called a **reeve**, watched over the serfs to make sure they worked hard and followed the noble's orders.

▼ WORKING THE LAND
In the Middle Ages, life was difficult. Because everything had to be produced by hand, most peasants were forced to farm the land and harvest the grain.

Protecting the Peasants

Ordinary people in the Middle Ages led very simple lives. Serfs had few luxuries and spent little time resting. But during periods of fighting, serfs enjoyed the protection of the lord, who lived in the largest house in the kingdom.

The reeve watched the serfs and checked their work.

Wheat was the main crop in northern Europe and was used to make bread.

These serfs used a curved blade called a sickle to cut the wheat stalks.

Villages Under Attack

Villages were designed to protect people against attack. The ordinary houses and the farm buildings were built inside a high fence, in a yard known as a **bailey**. A high mound of earth, or **motte**, was piled up

◄ PROTECTED BY THE CASTLE
This illustration from a medieval calendar shows serfs plowing the fields in front of the largest castle in France.

A high outer wall with tall wooden gates kept most attackers away.

Serfs planted crops and used oxen to plow the fields.

Houses, barns, and sometimes a chapel were built inside the bailey.

The **drawbridge** was lifted if an enemy attacked.

xt to the bailey. The lord's **keep**, or
ain house, was built on top. If the
ngdom came under attack, villagers
ould move into the keep for safety. The
rd and the adult men would go out to
eet the attackers, or prepare the house
r defense. The keep also contained
pplies of food and drink. This helped
e villagers to stay alive inside the keep if
e attack lasted a long time.

The keep was where the
lord and his family lived.

▼ MOTTE-AND-BAILEY
This model shows what a typical
motte-and-bailey castle looked like.

A drop-down gate
was lifted once
everyone was safe at
the top of the motte.

A fence and **moat**
surrounded the
motte and bailey.

Steep sides were
difficult for an
enemy to climb.

CHAPTER 3

Knights of the Crusades

The Crusades were a long series of wars fought by Christian armies. The wars were approved of by the Pope. They were fought against Muslims in the Holy Land, the region known today as the Middle East.

Many knights traveled to the Holy Land hoping to achieve success and gain wealth. Other knights believed that their sins would be forgiven if they defended the Holy Land from Muslim forces.

▼ MEDIEVAL EUROPE

Knights made long, expensive voyages from Europe to take part in Crusades, traveling across land and over seas. Many would never return. This map shows regions from where the knights traveled as well as the location of the Holy Land.

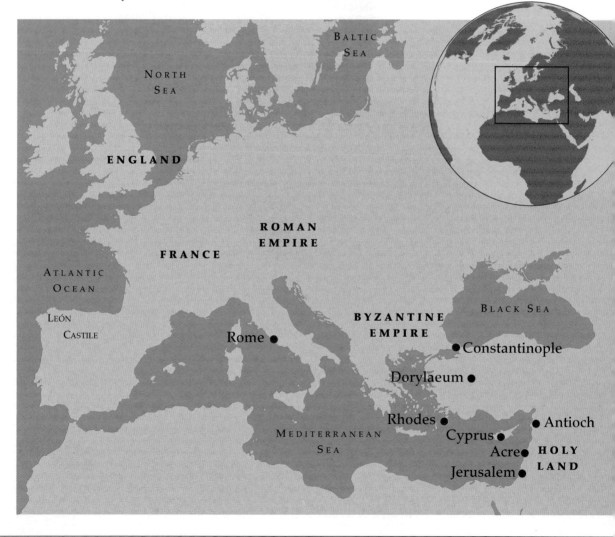

CRUSADER BATTLE
This image shows a battle between Crusader Knights and Seljuk Turks during the First Crusade (1096–1099). Christian forces won battles at Dorylaeum (Door-ee-LAY-um) and Antioch (AN-tee-ock) and recaptured much of the Holy Land.

Some knights stayed in the Holy Land to protect areas captured by Christian armies. Those knights formed special orders, or brotherhoods. They adopted specific rules and led religious lives.

Knights Hospitaller

Italian merchants built the hospital of St. John of Jerusalem in the 1000s. It was for Christian **pilgrims** visiting the Holy Land. Some crusader knights who arrived in

Jerusalem promised themselves to the hospital. They cared for sick or poor pilgrims. They wanted to hold Christian-occupied lands and defend them from attack. These knights formed the Knights of St. John of Jerusalem, or the Knights Hospitaller.

▶ KNIGHTS TEMPLAR
This painting from the 1300s shows two Knights Templar wearing chain mail and helmets. They are approaching the open gates of the city of Jerusalem, overlooked by three Muslim warriors.

▼ PALACE OF THE GRAND MASTER
After Jerusalem was captured by Muslim forces, the Knights Hospitaller moved to Rhodes, Greece. They built this massive castle, the Palace of the Grand Master of the Knights of Rhodes.

Knights Templar

The Order of the Knights Templar was formed in the early 1100s to protect Christian pilgrims. The crusaders promised to live in poverty. They were given a place to live in Jerusalem that had once been a Jewish temple.

Over the years, along with the Knights Hospitaller, the Knights Templar became one of the richest and most powerful organizations in Europe. In addition to protecting Christians, they also became bankers. They even owned the island of Cyprus. By the 1200s, however, the Knights Templar had become unpopular with European kings and the Pope. Nobles believed the Knights Templar had become too powerful. Members of the group were **persecuted**. Their leaders were executed. The order was completely outlawed by the Pope in 1312.

Teutonic Knights

Crusaders attacked the city of Acre (in present-day Israel) in 1190. During the siege, some German merchants set up a hospital. They founded a new German order of knights known as the Teutonic Knights. In the 1200s, after Christian armies had been defeated in the Holy Land, the Teutonic Knights moved to eastern Europe. They wanted to convert the **pagan** tribes there to Christianity—by force if necessary.

This type of helmet was known as a **great helm.** It covered the head completely, but it was heavy and uncomfortable.

Chain mail protected knights from attackers' swords. Crusader knights had flags on their lances to show they were Christians.

The cross of the Knights Hospitaller helped to identify the knight in battle.

A long sword was the crusader knight's main weapon.

Crusaders' horses were not usually armored— transporting horse armor across Europe would have been too expensive.

▲ A CRUSADER KNIGHT
This Knight Hospitaller was one of thousands of knights who traveled to the Holy Land. Knights from this group fought against Muslim forces and occupied the Holy Lands during the Crusades.

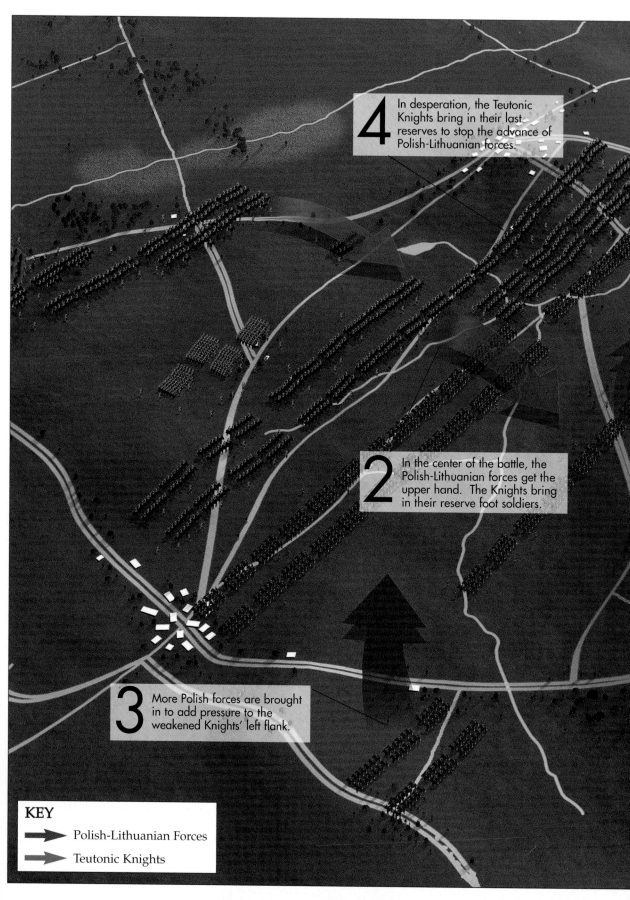

4 In desperation, the Teutonic Knights bring in their last reserves to stop the advance of Polish-Lithuanian forces.

2 In the center of the battle, the Polish-Lithuanian forces get the upper hand. The Knights bring in their reserve foot soldiers.

3 More Polish forces are brought in to add pressure to the weakened Knights' left flank.

KEY

Polish-Lithuanian Forces

Teutonic Knights

Battle of Grunwald
July 15, 1410

The Battle of Grunwald was one of the largest battles of the Middle Ages. By the early 1400s, the powerful Teutonic Knights had taken over much of Eastern Europe. They threatened to overrun Poland and Lithuania, which were then united as one kingdom. The Teutonic Knights were joined by other Christian knights from across Europe. They began their crusade in order to convert the pagan peoples of Lithuania and Poland to Christianity, yet they were after their land, too.

Teutonic Defeat

The Teutonic Knights met the Polish-Lithuanian forces near a Polish village called Grunwald. The German knights were in for a shock. The Polish-Lithuanian forces were strengthened by mercenaries and Tartar horsemen from Russia. The German knights were overpowered. Their leaders were slaughtered. The Battle of Grunwald ended the Teutonic Order's power in Eastern Europe.

1 Lithuanian fighters on horseback attack the Teutonic foot soldiers. They are beaten back by German knights.

5 The Polish king throws in his last reserves. To their right, the Lithuanian horsemen return to the battle. The Teutonic Knights have no foot soldiers left and are defeated by the larger Polish-Lithuanian forces.

CHAPTER 4

A Knight's Armor

In the early Middle Ages, even simple armor was very expensive. It took a long time to make. Chain mail protected against slashing swords, but it was uncomfortable. Knights had to wear padded shirts under chain mail to prevent their bodies from being cut by the armor.

Apart from his armor, a knight's main protection was his shield. Early wooden shields were large. As body armor improved shields became smaller and lighter. They were usually fitted with a strap that went around the neck, leaving a knight's hands free. A metal "boss" made the shield stronger

▶ SUIT OF ARMOR
Knights often wore both chain mail and armor. Together they weighed about 60 pounds (27 kg). This combination helped knights to fight on foot and horseback.

Eye slits helped the knight see. An attacker could kill the knight by sticking a dagger through the helmet's slits, however.

Chain mail was better than armor around the neck. Unlike plate armor, chain mail enabled the knight to move freely.

Gauntlets were made of many pieces to allow the proper grip of weapons.

Long swords like this one were used for blocking, stabbing, and slashing enemies.

Daggers were useful for close combat.

Armor was flexible at knee and elbow joints.

Scale and Plate Armor

Some of the earliest armored knights were those of the Byzantine (BIZ-zan-teen) Empire. This was once the eastern half of the old Roman Empire. The Byzantine Empire ruled much of the Holy Land and parts of eastern Europe. It was in power until the fall of its capital, Constantinople (present-day Istanbul, Turkey), in 1453. Byzantine horsemen fought covered in small metal scales, called **scale armor**.

DID YOU KNOW?

Armor styles advanced during the Middle Ages, but armor is not a medieval invention. The first use of armor dates back to ancient times. It was sometimes worn by Roman soldiers.

Chain mail covered the Byzantine horseman's face.

Layers of armor called scales were made by hammering thin sheets of metal into a shape like a scoop.

▶ BYZANTINE HORSEMAN
In the early 1100s, Byzantine horsemen and their horses wore scale armor. In the heat of the Holy Land, this would have been hot and uncomfortable.

Scale armor was sewn onto a backing cloth.

Plate armor was stronger than scale armor. It was developed to protect knights from powerful **crossbows** and early firearms that were in use by the 1300s. Based on scale armor, plate armor was quickly adopted. Then it was improved on by Europeans. Plate armor was made of solid plates of metal. They overlapped and were loosely joined to allow knights to move freely. But plate armor was heavier than chain mail. Armor makers tested the strength of the best plate armor by firing a crossbow or pistol at it from a close range.

Armor makers also made plate armor for horses. By the 1400s, the necks, chests, and sides of horses were usually well protected. That meant that knights had to have bigger, stronger horses to hold up the added weight.

Styles of Armor

There were different fashions in armor, too. Suits of armor made for kings and princes were often decorated with gold and silver. Long, pointed shoes were sometimes worn, but were removed for riding.

◄ HENRY VIII'S ARMOR
This suit of armor was made for Henry VIII of England in 1515.

Helmets

Early helmets were simple. They consisted of a tightly fitted cap of metal or leather. Many knights also had hoods and collars of chain mail to protect their necks.

For most of the Middle Ages, large helmets covered the entire head and face. One early helmet was known as a great helm. It was worn at the beginning of a battle when knights charged at each other with lances.

Great helms limited a knight's vision. They were also heavy, so many knights removed them for close combat. Some knights wore smaller, simpler helmets called **basinets**. By the 1300s, most knights wore basinet helmets. Many basinets had a metal visor that could be lifted during battle in order to see.

In Their Own Words

"What is the function of knights? To guard the Church, to fight unbelievers…and if need be, to lay down their lives."

—John of Salisbury, *Policraticus*, 1159

▶ FULL–FACE HELMET
This basinet was the most common type worn by knights in the 1300s.

Visors at the front of the helmet were usually hinged so the wearer could lift them to see better.

Swords slid off pointed helmets without harming the head.

Chain mail was attached to the helmet or worn inside it as a hood to protect the neck.

Helmets with pointed visors were called "dog-faced" helmets.

CHAPTER 5

Life off the Battlefield

Off the battlefield, medieval knights and other soldiers lived in field camps. Often these camps were elaborate, with brightly colored tents. Still, even with the brightest colors, camp life was unpleasant. It was often either too hot or too cold in the tents. Food sometimes smelled foul. It was cooked on smoky fires that burned the eyes.

Heralds and Coats of Arms

During a battle, **heralds** took messages from one part of the field to another. After the battle ended, the heralds took on the grim task of identifying the dead knights. The king or lord was interested only in how many noble knights he lost. Foot soldiers or peasants were less important to him.

A horn was used to signal the start of a battle.

This herald wears a close-fitted jacket and leggings. Most medieval clothing was made of wool or linen.

▶ MEDIEVAL HERALD
Heralds were messengers, not soldiers. They carried letters between leaders when the leaders wanted to make peace or declare war. If a knight was captured, the herald would agree on a ransom, or a sum of money to be paid for the knight's release.

cause knights in similar armor were hard
identify, they began wearing special
mbols. Knights within the same order
ore the same designs on their armor,
othes, and shields. This made them
sier to pick out both during and after a
ttle. These "coats of arms" were passed
n from father to son. The son might also
ld his own symbols to the coat of arms.
hey often became highly decorated.

The castle was the symbol
of the Kingdom of Castile.

The lion was the symbol of
the Kingdom of León.

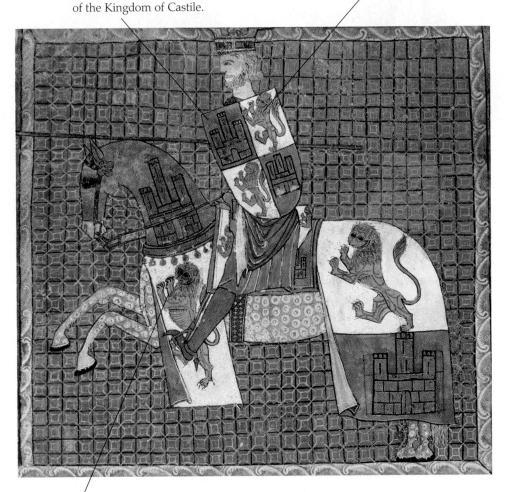

The cloth cover on a fighting
horse was called a caparison.

▲ COAT OF ARMS
This medieval illustration shows King Alfonso X of
Castile and León, now part of present-day Spain. He
displays his family coat of arms on his shield and on his
horse's **caparison**.

These knights took part in a jousting tournament. Their lances have just made contact. Their horses reared up on their hind legs because of the force of the blow. Jousting was a dangerous sport.

The first heralds were probably wandering **minstrels** or storytellers. They needed to have sharp minds in order to remember songs. A good memory was also useful for remembering who wore which coat of arms. Heralds were treated with great respect. They granted coats of arms and kept historical records.

Tournaments

Knights needed to practice fighting when they were not actually in battle. To do so, they took part in tournaments. These were "war games" in which knights fought each other to practice and show off their fighting skills. Tournaments were often organized by heralds. There might be a number of events in a tournament including mock battles and jousting. Jousting was when individual knights tried to knock each other off their horses with lances. They charged each other at great speed. Such contests could be very dangerous. Lances for jousting were more blunt than those

ctually used in battle. Even so, knights
were sometimes injured or even killed in
jousting matches. While they were away
from home, but not fighting, knights
sometimes organized their own jousting
matches. Kings disapproved of these. They
were afraid they might lose some of their
best knights before the next battle.

▼ CAMP LIFE

When away from home, armies lived in camps,
sometimes for years. Servants competed for the best
place to pitch their master's tent, and sometimes had
fights of their own! A knight would often share his
tent with his horse.

Tents were made from fabric
hung over wooden poles.

ood was cooked
ver wood fires.

Trunks or chests contained
everything a knight carried
with him.

Barrels were filled with
food and drink.

Donkeys were used
for carrying baggage.

"When the tournament was in progress, knights… fell in such numbers… that it seemed the sport not so much of men [but] of demons."

—Thomas of Cantimpré describing a jousting tournament at Neuss, Germany, 1241

Jousting offered knights an opportunity to impress female spectators. Knights often wore a sleeve or another personal item given to them by a lady. They promised to compete in the joust for that lady's honor and to win her respect.

The Knights' Code

On the battlefield or off it, knights were supposed to follow a set of rules. This was called the **chivalric** (shiv-AL-rik) **code**. This code instructed a knight to respect God and his fellow countrymen. It instructed knights to be brave and honest at times of war and peace. The chivalric code expected knights to help the poor and weak.

The code barred a knight from killing another knight if it could be avoided. Instead, a defeated knight was held for ransom. Abuse such as knocking out a prisoner's teeth in order to get a higher ransom was also forbidden.

◄ PRIZED GIFT
This painting shows a noble lady giving a ring to a knight. It was either to carry as her favor, or as a reward for winning.

Arthur was a legendary king of England.

The Holy Grail was featured in many stories about King Arthur. It is said to be the cup used by Jesus at the Last Supper.

The round table showed that all of the knights were equal. No one knight was seated in a place of higher power.

KNIGHTS OF THE ROUND TABLE

The stories of King Arthur and his knights have been told since medieval times. Even in the 1400s when this painting was made, nobody knew whether famous knights such as Sir Lancelot and Sir Gawain ever existed.

Courtly Love

Another part of the chivalric code described courtly love. Knights were expected to respect women, act bravely in their honor, and admire them from a distance.

The most famous example of courtly love is the fictional story of King Arthur's favorite knight, Lancelot, and Arthur's queen, Guinevere. Unfortunately the romance developed into real love, which the chivalric code did not permit. The scandal ruined the friendship between Lancelot and Sir Gawain. It eventually brought about the end of King Arthur's court. Stories like that of Lancelot and Guinevere were told to reinforce the importance of living within the rules of the chivalric code.

The age of the medieval knight came to an end around the time the handgun was invented. Modern firearms forever changed medieval fighting techniques. Still, the romantic stories about knights live on. Those stories ensure that knights will never be forgotten. Their medieval world was much harsher than the one described in stories, however.

Glossary

bailey—the space enclosed by the outer wall or fence of a motte-and-bailey castle

basinets—close-fitting metal helmets with visors

caparison—a horse's cloth cover, usually decorated with the coat of arms of a knight

chain mail—a type of armor made of many small metal rings linked together

chaplain—a member of the Christian Church who served a household

chivalric code—a set of religious, moral, and social rules followed by medieval knights

citadel—a fortified building

crossbows—small bows with instruments for drawing and releasing the strings

Crusades—a series of military expeditions made by European Christians to the Middle East to fight against Muslims and recover the Holy Land

drawbridge—a wooden platform or bridge to a castle entrance that spans a moat or water, which can be raised to block people from entering

feudal system—a medieval social system consisting of a king, lords, vassals, knights, peasants, and serfs. Vassals and knights pledged their loyalty to lords and fought in wars for them, in return for protection and land. Peasants and serfs were bound to farm this land and were given a share of the food produced on it.

fief—land given by a lord to a vassal under the feudal system, in return for the vassal's military service and loyalty

flank—the side of a military or naval formation

gauntlet—an armored glove

great helm—a one-piece metal helmet covering the entire head

hauberks—knee-length shirts of chain mail

herald—an official messenger who carried messages between a king and his nobles on the battlefield

keep—fortified building in which a noble and his family lived

knight—a medieval soldier who was specially trained to fight on horseback

lance—a long wooden weapon with a pointed tip, used by soldiers on horseback

mercenary—a soldier who is paid to fight

minstrels—traveling entertainers who performed music, songs, and poetry

moat—a wide, deep ditch, often filled with water, dug around a castle, fortress, or walled town to provide protection

motte—an artificial mound of earth on which a keep was built

noble—a member of the wealthy ruling class

pagan—a person who does not believe in a single god but instead worships a number of nature gods or spirits

page—a young boy in training to become a knight and who served as a knight's assistant

persecuted—cruelly treated or punished, often for religious reasons

pilgrims—religious people who travel to a place or shrine important to their faith

plate armor—protective covering made up of large metal plates designed to be worn on the chest, arms and legs

pronounced—made an official or formal statement

reeve—the local manager of a lord's manor house and land

rituals—ceremonies practiced in the same way

scale armor—armor or protective clothing made up of many small metal or leather plates attached to cloth or leather

serfs—members of the lowest class under the feudal system who were required to work on a noble's land in return for food

sheath—a covering for a sword or dagger blade

squire—a young adult man working for a knight who was training to become a knight himself

vassals—people who were given protection and sometimes land by a lord, in return for their loyalty and military service

visor—the part of a helmet that protects the face

For More Information

Books

rms & Armor. Eyewitness Books (series). ...ichele Byam (DK Publishing, 2004)

...ight. Eyewitness Books (series). ...ristopher Gravett (DK Publishing, 2007)

...ights, Castles, and Warfare in the Middle Ages. ...orld Almanac Library of the Middle Ages ...eries). Fiona MacDonald (World Almanac ...brary, 2005)

...nights: Warriors of the Middle Ages. High ...terest Books (series). Aileen Weintraub ...hildren's Press, 2005)

...edieval Warfare. Medieval World (series). ...ra Steele (Crabtree Publishing, 2003)

Web Sites

...astle & Siege Terminology
...tp://home.olemiss.edu/~tjray/medieval/castle.htm
...earch a glossary of terms that describes the ...atures of medieval castles and fortresses. ...nd out about turrets, parapets, weapons, ...nd more.

Castles of Britain: Castle Learning Center
http://www.castles-of-britain.com/castle6.htm
Tour this fascinating site that contains articles, photographs, artwork, and diagrams explaining medieval life, including information about knights and weaponry.

The Medieval World: Medieval Battles
http://medieval.etrusia.co.uk/battles
Learn more about medieval England, its castles, knights, warfare, and the Crusades.

The Middle Ages
http://www.learner.org/interactives/middleages
Charge through this site and learn about the feudal system, religion, castles, clothing, and the arts.

The Middle Ages: The Medieval Knight
http://library.thinkquest.org/10949/fief/medknight.html
Review information about becoming a medieval knight, including sections about armor, weapons, tournaments, and codes of chivalry and conduct.

Index